D1307263

FIRST LOOK

UNDER THE SEA

For a free color catalog describing Gareth Stevens' list of high-quality children's books, call 1-800-341-3569 (USA) or 1-800-461-9120 (Canada).

Library of Congress Cataloging-in-Publication Data

Llewellyn, Claire.
    First look under the sea / Claire Llewellyn.
      p. cm. — (First look)
    "North American edition"—T.p. verso.
    Includes bibliographical references and index.
    Summary: An introduction to the diverse life forms living in the oceans. Also
discusses fuel from the sea, sea food, and pollution of the oceans.
    ISBN 0-8368-0702-2
    1. Marine biology—Juvenile literature. 2. Marine resources—Juvenile literature.
[1. Marine biology. 2. Marine resources.] I. Title. II. Series.
QH91.16.L54 1991
574.92—dc20   91-9418

North American edition first published in 1991 by
Gareth Stevens Children's Books
1555 North RiverCenter Drive, Suite 201
Milwaukee, Wisconsin 53212, USA

U.S. edition copyright © 1991 by Gareth Stevens, Inc. First published as *Under the Sea* in the United Kingdom, copyright © 1991, by Simon & Schuster Young Books. Additional end matter copyright © 1991 by Gareth Stevens, Inc.

Photograph credits: Heather Angel, 24, 26; Liz and Tony Bomford/ARDEA LONDON, 15; Konrad Wothe/Bruce Coleman Limited, 16; ZEFA, all others
Line artwork: Raymond Turvey

Series editor: Patricia Lantier-Sampon
Design: M&M Design Partnership
Cover design: Laurie Shock
Layout: Sharone Burris

Printed in the United States of America

1 2 3 4 5 6 7 8 9 97 96 95 94 93 92 91

FIRST LOOK

CLAIRE LLEWELLYN

UNDER THE SEA

Gareth Stevens Children's Books

MILWAUKEE

CONTENTS

WHERE LAND MEETS SEA

Have you ever been to the seashore? Did you see any of the creatures that live there? Where were they? Did you know what they were?

Why do you think so many creatures on the shore live inside shells?

7

DARKNESS UNDER THE SEA

We begin each new morning with daylight. There are so many things to see and hear.

Is there light under the sea? How do divers see in very deep water? What sounds might they hear?

AT HOME IN THE SEA

Thousands of fish, other animals, and plants live in the sea. Some are so small that you cannot even see them.

Can you guess which are the largest creatures in the sea?

11

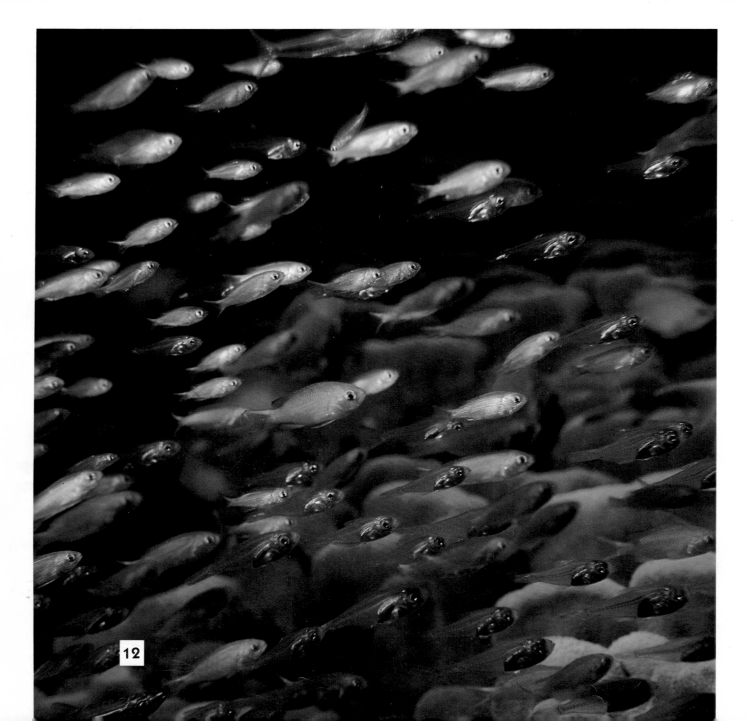

12

FISH NEED TO PROTECT THEMSELVES

There are thousands of different kinds of fish in the sea — fish of every color and size.

Fish sometimes prey on each other. Can you think of ways that fish try to protect themselves against enemies?

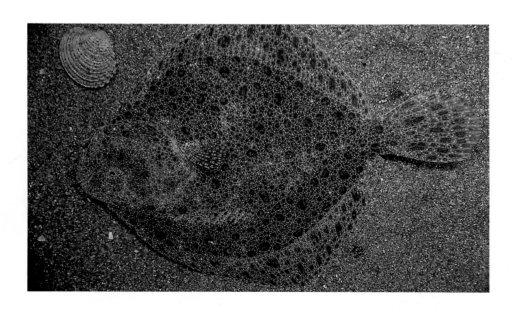

STREAMLINED FOR THE SEA

Have you ever tried to catch a fish in a stream or pond with your hands? Was it easy?

How does the shape of a fish's body help it move through water?

Many animals are streamlined for life in the sea. Can you describe how seals look when they move on land? How do they look when they move in water?

15

16

FOOD FOR ANIMALS

Many animals that don't live in the sea depend on it for their food.

Have you ever seen birds dive into the sea for fish? How do they know where the fish are? Do you wish you could dive like that?

FOOD FOR PEOPLE

Every morning and evening, fishermen around the world work hard to catch fish, shrimp, and other seafood. This can be a dangerous job.

How many different ways of fishing can you think of? Have you tried any of them?

19

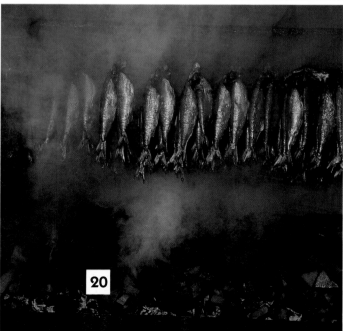

20

BUYING AND SELLING FISH

Fishermen sell their catch at a market or other places. Sometimes the market or shops may be a long way from the docks. What kinds of things do you think the fishermen can do to keep the fish fresh?

Do you eat fish at your house? Where do you buy it? What kinds of fish do you like best?

FUEL FROM THE SEA

It's not just food that we take from the sea. Look at the picture of the oil rig. Why has it been built in the middle of the sea? Do you think there is oil beneath the sea?

Working on an oil rig can be dangerous. Why is oil so important to us?

23

SEA POLLUTION

What does the sea look like when it is polluted? How does this happen?

What do you think happens to tiny sea creatures when the water is polluted? What happens to the fish, birds, and other animals that feed on them?

BREATHING UNDER THE SEA

Do you ever swim underwater? How long can you hold your breath? How does it feel?

Some animals that live in the sea can't breathe underwater, either. Can you name some of them?

How do divers breathe under the sea?

STORIES FROM UNDER THE SEA

People have sailed the sea for hundreds of years. Sometimes their ships sank. Can you think of some reasons why?

Divers try to find old shipwrecks resting on the seabed. Have you ever heard of or read about any famous shipwrecks?

Can we learn anything from these wrecks?

More Books about the Sea

Animals of Sea and Shore. Podendorf (Childrens Press)
At the Beach. Booth (Raintree)
At the Beach. Rockwell (Macmillan)
Creatures of the Sea. (Price Stern)
A Day at the Beach. Vasiliu (Random House)
From Sea to Salt. Mitgutsch (Carolrhoda Books)
Let's Discover the Sea. (Raintree)
Let's Take a Walk on the Beach. O'Connor (Child's World)
The Seaside. Rius and Parramon (Barron's Educational Series)
Starfish. Hurd (Harper & Row Junior Books)
Under the Sea. Thompson and Overbeck (Lerner Publications)
What's for Lunch? The Eating Habits of Seashore Creatures. Epstein (Macmillan)
What's under the Sea? Russell (Abingdon)
Wonders of the Sea. Sabin (Troll Associates)

Glossary

Diver: A person who explores or works underwater. Divers often work around ships that have sunk to the bottom of the sea.

Dock: A place where boats can be put into the water. Docks are also places where boats can land and stay safely tied until the next fishing or boating trip.

Market: A place where people can go to buy and sell food, clothing, and other types of goods.

Pollute: To make something dirty. Pollution in the sea poisons the plants and animals that live there.

Pond: A small body of water. Fish and frogs are two types of animals that can live in ponds.

Prey: An animal that is hunted or caught by another for food; also, to hunt or go after something in an attempt to attack or capture it.

Seabed: The very bottom, or floor, of the ocean or sea. When ships sink, they most often drop down to the seabed.

Seal: An animal with flippers that lives in the water. Most seals live in cold regions of the world.

Shell: The outer case, or covering, of a small water animal. Clams, shrimp, crabs, and lobsters are some sea animals that have shells.

Shipwreck: A ship that has been destroyed or wrecked. Badly damaged ships usually sink to the bottom of the sea.

Shore: The land that goes around, or surrounds, a body of water. Boats usually dock on the shoreline.

Streamlined: Having a shape designed to move easily through water or air. Fish and seals have streamlined bodies that allow them to swim quickly.

Index

A number that is in **boldface** type means that the page has a picture of the subject on it.

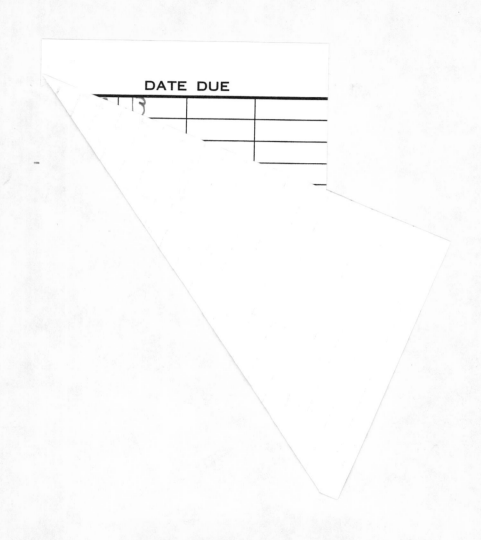

DATE DUE